WITHDRAWN

T5-ANV-570

necessary kindling

poems

necessary kindling

anjail rashida ahmad

Louisiana State)|(*University Press*   *baton rouge*   2001

Copyright © 1990, 1992, 1995, 1996, 1999, 2001 by Anjail Rashida Ahmad
All rights reserved
Manufactured in the United States of America
First printing
10   09   08   07   06   05   04   03   02   01
5   4   3   2   1

Designer: Amanda McDonald
Typeface: Bembo
Printer and binder: Thomson-Shore, Inc.

Library of Congress Cataloging-in-Publication Data:

Ahmad, Anjail Rashida.
    Necessary kindling : poems / Anjail Rashida Ahmad.
        p. cm.
    ISBN 0-8071-2713-2 (alk. paper) — ISBN 0-8071-2714-0 (pbk. : alk. paper)
    1. African American women—Poetry. I. Title.
    PS3551.H68 N43 2001
        811'.6 — dc21
00-012948

The author gratefully acknowledges the editors of the following publications, in which some of the poems in this book first appeared, sometimes in slightly different form: *African American Review:* "namesake"; *All That Jazz:* "atoning"; *Black Scholar:* "atoning"; *Midlands:* "what some women wear in their bones," "on the fire trail"; *Washington Square Review:* "breach"; and *Writer's Festival Magazine:* "sunday," "thorn in the side of the rose."

I offer my gratitude to my family and friends who have beamed their love toward me my whole life. And to the Unseen Hosts who accompany me at every turn, whispering and nudging, singing the lyrics, helping me fill every line.

I give a special thanks to the staff at Louisiana State University Press for their belief in and support of my work. An additional thanks goes to my editor, George Roupe, for his tireless efforts toward achieving perfection.

A special nod of appreciation goes to poet Pinkie Gordon Lane, who pushed the doors of opportunity open wide for another sister poet. Thank you.

Thanks also to Dr. Patricia E. Bonner, Dr. Steve Guthrie, and Dr. Geta Leseur, who have mentored me and held my hand and have done whatever was necessary to keep me in the "game."

Thanks to Cynthia Cole for contributing the cover design.

The paper in this book meets the guidelines for permanence and durability of the Committee on Production Guidelines for Book Longevity of the Council on Library Resources. ∞

For my mother, Carolyn, and my father, Almond.

and for my children:

Sulaiman, Munirah and Safiya. and the next generation:

Micah, Asha and Zarinah, the new Light in my life.

I also dedicate this volume to the memory of my

great grandmother: Grandma Berry,

daughter of the Spirit, 1884–1959,

and to my grandmother, who loved me beyond

measure: Marguerite Caroline Berry Hall,

1913–1987.

we are all here now.

contents

necessary kindling

the poet

> each morning i pull myself
> out of despair . . .
>> —lucille clifton, *book of light*

each night, she climbs
     with the bulb of her body
to the room at the top of the house
where she lies down in the dark
trellis of her bed.

her dreams gather,
  in the mouths of ancestors,
              whispering the bitter code
of what is possible.

when she awakens,
she remembers
the shape of her own breath,
pressing it
     into the heart of her words.

thorn in the side of the rose

for America Anna Elizabeth Goode Berry (1884–1959)

i wonder what it would be like to talk
with you now, great-grandmother.
i barely knew you before you died.
i remember the scent of rotting flesh singeing,
jaundiced wallpaper and the taste of apple jelly.

i remember your pain-riddled face
cradling distant eyes, a pain-stained smile.
i recall your kitchen table's smooth wood grain
graced by your veined hand, the brown
potbellied teapot flecked with reddish leaves,
and the smell of your life burning on the bone.

what would it be like to talk
with you now, great-grandmother—
i barely knew you before you died,
a secreted death, secluded in the upper
room of your daughter's house, the room
great-grandchildren would fill with boisterous lives
and raucous laughter long after you were gone.

you left without my knowing. you slipped
from the crumpled sheets and cancer-wasted body,
pouring through the mortar,
                              never looking back.

i study your sepia-edged photograph,
the whitened tufts: straight, without curl.
the quiet dignity of your eyes, and the soft cheeks
mounded above your slight, almost, smile.

i imagine your body a melon, opened
to six strong vines, the length of your life.
like any fruit, you yielded
to the husbandman of your life,
the calls for sex on demand,
the meals just as regular and the childfruit
sucking and draining you through the vine.

you wrote what you could of bibled verse,
laboring over those metered phrases
as if they were way stations
to gather your life about you.

America Anna Elizabeth Goode Berry,
wife of Andrew, daughter of Caroline and Amos,
what would you say to your tertiary generation—

if prayers answer like a voiceless wind,
then i imagine it's you
stirring me to lamplight and pen
in the early margins of morning.

what some women wear in their bones

she sang
about what crowned her,
what it was that made her,
and others of her generation, *a woman.*
she said she *was lucky to have married
some fifty years ago.*

> *in my day,
> a woman was prized
> for her strong bones,
> her steady gaze,
> her pleasant disposition, and hair
> that lifted like glory toward heaven.*

in the shifting light,
her proud bones softened
beneath blemished patches of skin
stretched over her broad, dished-out face
and the curvature of forearms muscled
from hoisting pots, lifting baskets of laundry
and balancing babies on her hips.

she crossed her arms under her breast as we paused
in the clearing. the sky sifted purplish blue
above pine boughs and the dull nodes of heads bound
                                        by marriage.

bound by blood
is what she said over and over into the evening
air. she kept repeating it like a lyric
set loose from the strains of a now meaningless song
that turns on its own axis inside the opaque bone of the head
where notions of self are kept, where careless misgivings
can crowd the least developed sense
                        of one's worth.

                into the furrowed night,
she carried the long harp of her bones
hardened like the inner shell

of an unobtrusive mollusk
singing to itself
in the wet dark of a riverbed,
layering over its bitter bulb of sand,
its miracle of milky stone,
the heart of *a pearl borne at great price.*

in these still vital moments

my mom, her rubied eyes glistening,
stood out from among
the other women. this is evident

even though the once glossy
photos in the family album
are wearing thin.

today on this visit,
though she has had a great spirit
for persevering, i can see
she is tired now.

   this is a poor season for my regrets—

in a few days, my mother will become the eldest
matriarch,
   the eldest mediator of family ills.
    Aunt R. will pass away from liver cancer—

tomorrow, we will visit Aunt R. at the hospital.
i will apprentice at the foot of the bed,
watching from behind, as my mom ministers to her
elder, feeding her fruit and deliberate conversation.
she wants to keep Aunt R. in these still vital moments . . .

   lord, will the circle be unbroken
        by and by—
witnessing these two
do what women of my family have always done,
i begin to understand
   what i've taken for granted
all the years before:
how the acts of women—
      loving themselves—
can keep the spirit
    renewed.

on the day after . . .

for Marguerite Berry Hall (1913–1987)

the day you left your body
i remembered the poet musing about the *Soul,*
   something about what the *Soul* selects—

     can't say i know what it is
i choose
in this chary light   shadow of flame
       ascending
black-lipped wick

each day
  i awaken from fitful sleep
more tired than before.

. . . would i choose to remain
        in this
stint of darkness   this let of light
where bones
     roam
   the charnel houses—

without
the glint of day
that bares its teeth
     without hesitation,
how would i know you were ever here—

here   at the edge   of my body
at the exact spot
where the *Soul* is said to
  come and go at will.
           i wait . . .

when will i have the choice
to leave at my leisure—

when will the stealthy winged
Soul demure in its posture

                    stop the charade
with its sideways
                    hopscotch
from one life to the next   hardly ever stopping
long enough   to pick up the scatter—

namesake

Names do give humans power over what they name. . . .
—Walter Ong, *Orality and Literacy*

my daughter sits on the couch, a totem
doll with the bell of her womb jutting
                              below her ribs.
she is clanged full of child.

its life sprouts like an inverted flower,
the genus geranium:
cranesbill, storksbill, so named
for the elongated shape of its fruit.

my daughter knows her history.
she's naming her own fruit
according to the shape of our lives.
she's following in the footsteps
of her ancestors, weaving the warp of the generations
through the passage of names
from the past to the future, present with us.

she's following a tradition
that women in our family have kept alive
for at least six generations: the art of gifting a girl-
child with a part of her own name
or one from an auntie, grandma or favored cousin.

what power this calling forth of the past
into the present, this reaffirming the female life,
the durability of the clan
peopled by so many strong-wombed women.

i did not keep our tradition alive,
did not mark the fruit of my womb
with the powerful totem of a renamed name.
                              and like a loose strand
or one that has missed its loop altogether,
my daughter pulls me back.

she's giving part of my name to her own child,
looping us into that intricate tapestry of women's names
singing themselves.

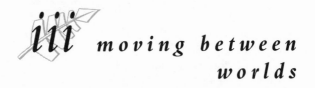

iii *moving between worlds*

in late august before sputnik orbits its great metallic eye over the earth

Cincinnati, Ohio, 1957

this saturday evening shimmers
her skirts just outside
the living-room window
for the brown-skinned dancers
shimmying and strutting around the floor,
heads tossed back, eyes closed against the light
while their tongues say *ah-h.*
done with serving the white folk, the men don
smooth cotton shirts with bright
tie tacks and silken handkerchiefs
taunting the lips of their suit pockets,
a bourbon, jigged with ice, in one hand,
the other slippered
inside a trouser pocket for the sake of style.
like the men, the women's heads
glisten with a pomade shine
while their full-bottomed skirts
and off-the-shoulder blouses
would make them the talk of the town
if they could make their promenade on main street.
but in these two basement rooms,
transformed for the night
into a momentary paradise,
it's a strange moon that bows
as bill doggett plays
        his funky *honky-tonk*
            for this round of swaying bodies
        saying *yes sir* and *no ma'am*
only to themselves, wanting
the night to last a little longer,

forestalling sunday's bus ride
to the carlsons' or the wilseys',
where they must glide in through back doors
on invisible feet and with heads
bowed, slightly, when saying
yes sir and *yes ma'am*
while their eyes are saying *no.*

the griot brings us the blues and lifts us into the realm of jazz

after the forced voyages
of the african, bound
and carried like cargo,
it begins—

the soul of the griot
                reworking
the five-tone scale.

that new negro
half-stripped of her culture:
only the soul remains, remembers
the repetition of histories,
the marrow of her traditions.

oh,
master chanters,
recite the lines
of ancestral ascendancy
from the fields,
all the way to congo square.

new world griot,
climb the loins of your fathers;
sleep at the breasts of your mothers.
take hold of those deep-rooted vines.
holler across the fields. under threat of lash
and locust, assert yourself.
                climb with your music
                        to the mouth of god.

shout the cryptic.
chill the air
with breaking tones
and sliding notes.
rend the blue black misery;
raise it to the 5th side of heaven.

give us a tapestry
woven with your pain, your joy.
reach your god through song.

teach us, griot bluesman.
sing the underbelly of our pain.
teach us, griot blueswoman,
about the coming of sweet jesus;
sing us into oblivion.

play on, griot,
take the instruments of the blue eyes,
bend them, redefine them
along the lines of your soul.

take your five notes,
string them like jewels,
surround us with the heat of dixieland.

     beat it up,
    heat it up,
great gods of syncopation;
burn the way for the spontaneous:
                    the lords of the improv.

climb out of the furnace.
rag your notes all the way to sedalia.
heat up chicago and detroit,
blow clear to new york city,
innovating as you go,
as only you can.

swing, great griot,
blow into that horn,
        split atoms,
make new all things.

stride walk,
lift those keys,
raise the blues,
        make a new gospel.

        syncopate the melody—
    improvise the harmony—

burst the new world
        where negroes
reclaim roots
        become women,
reclaim roots
        become men,
where universe hangs a new left,
        and the whole world
seeks apprenticeship at your door.

a wound's deeper kiss

she stood admiring herself in the bathroom mirror,
gazing at the creamy hue of her skin, shaded, beneath
a budding crop of baby dreads. it was her hair that snared
her, drew her into a remembrance of her past, her long-ago
childhood, when the negroes, the coloreds, the pickaninnies
learned to place greater value on the silken headed and
lighter skinned among them. she remembered her grandmother,
a large woman of a nutmeg complexion, as such a one as these.

as slowly as a spring unwinds, her hair had begun to kink and curl,
to knot like a solidarity of nappy fists all over her head.
each matted dread had begun to thread into a promise of tomorrow.
each interwoven strand of her hair slid one over the other,
a scar, leaving a delicate memory of a wound's deeper kiss.

moving between worlds

at the gym today,
i glanced at a white woman
whose heavy frame slowed her stride.
we moved toward each other then looked away
as if caught by a fateful light.

it's murphy's law, she said in haste,
motioning toward the locker
where my belongings sat.
seeing her difficulty, i stepped aside.

at times like these,
        the old voice whispers:

                get back nigga', get back—

as if sensing my dis-ease
or perhaps thrown off by her own,

she proffers, *how long have you had your dreads—*
before i can answer, the old files shift into place
like deft dancers moving their slender figures across a waxed floor.

her query, is it sincere
or just brazen curiosity
toward what's perceived as strange or exotic—

my friend's dreads, she reports nervously, *are thick and long—*
*like knotty serpents—*with their bodies *splitting in two.*

       where is that self who has put away the suspicion of every white
                                     tongue—
i hear the moors went to ireland
                many years ago,
and that's where we get our curly hair . . .

                and what about the blacker the berry—

she flips her fingers through her reddish brown hair

humped in loose curls over her head. she
is not the worst case, she offers, *my father and brothers*
have it even more than me; only my mother has escaped.

i look at her pale skin
and try to imagine her large body
with some shade of blackened skin
and hair that kinks like a moor's might.
but from the tone of our conversation,
perhaps her hair would have been straightened
by a hot comb or the cruelest lye
as if that could have provided comfort
against the blackness of her skin
as she made reference to the luxury
of distant white relatives.

before long, i take leave for the upper floors
stretching in the full-length mirrors.
i study the wild branchings of my nappy dreads
and revel in the sheer pleasure of these kinky strands.
they have survived the middle passage, they have survived
the generation of slavery at the hands of the lustful white fathers.

the empty nest

Greenwich Village, N.Y., 1993

in the hovel of winter
night's pulse slows.
homeless men gather
on steaming grates
and in thick-lipped doorways. they dream
of burning the empty nest.

when the roof of winter breaks,
and the sun peels back a little of the cold,
they hold court on street corners,
toting bags and spewing their
ringed breaths into the air.

it's the grid of survival that they discuss,
ruminating about their journeys. holding
their histories up like maps, they read the legends,
and still no clear path shows through.

when the last of their hope has failed,
they cradle their penises
like diviners' rods,
piss against the buildings,
and watch as the thin-tailed streams
seep into the cracks
                    beneath their feet.

atoning

Washington, D.C., October 16, 1995

wanting or not, we watched the brilliant spectacle unfold
and swarm its hue around the capitol mall
as if filling the hull of a vast ship.
shipmates indeed, with nowhere to turn
except unto themselves.

and to themselves they turned,
like children, meeting for the first,
to exchange strange words
uttered from their hearts. this day,
there were no guns or knives, no words lifted to defame
nor to hide an inner pain of a self long despised.

at the feet of Lincoln and Jefferson, they confessed
the darkest lining of their souls,
all that they felt themselves to have done or not to have done,
wanting only to amend their ways,
wanting that slim chance to restore,
to lift up their lives like the newness of that day.

hear me. hear the voice of your family, my fathers,
brothers, uncles, and sons, stand-ins
for my own flesh and blood
who could not find their way into that place,
who could not have known, before they died,
that the tide, that awful tide
      that brought us to a darkening shore,
would be turned back, at last, for wider seas.

but there is no hope for them now
      except in you,
except that you
      fulfill the promise
                  you made.

afterglow

Harlem, N.Y., 1993

on stiver's row,
where tight-lipped terraces
whisper of the bygone—
harlem was a place of proud, bright people.

the heart of new york
thumped through her glory gates. poets, musicians
and long, lean dancers set a world on black fire—

but through my window,
the blown-out floors of a high-rise hawk
a purplish sky. the buildings
throw their cellar breaths onto the pavement.

almost everywhere,
evidence of death, and the dead
keep on dying
down on the corners
by the twos and threes: men
with their glassed-over eyes,
hands raised in half salute, shouting:
fuck it, fuck it, fuck you—

women,
draped in dull winter
coats, with hard hats of hair
cocked above the gleam
of their insatiable eyes,
drag the children,
push the strollers, curse
the burden of their motherhood.

—the eye can't help but cut itself
on their rough edges—

don't say manhattan—say harlem;
don't say new york apple—say cut off
   to the core;
       don't say tomorrow
when today is still the inside hull
     of a skeletal rind.

say life and mean death;
say death and mean despair.

the primary loss

New York City, July 1959

she stands,
with one foot raised
on the next to the highest step. her gloved hand
rests on her left knee, her right points down the shaft
of her hopeful body, every detail perfected:
the white, wide-brimmed straw hat with its ample shade, the pearls
knotted at the neck, the dress that doesn't reveal
and the aseptic gloves—

they were sticklers for the details in the '50s—

they stand atop the stairs,
bleached bare as bones, that lead
who knows where, and look more solid than the life
they've left behind . . . she and her postcard husband.
he is
in his own
photograph
complete with charcoal tones sooting out his roughest edges,
his manly-man gait that he swaggered in.

a dream can be had in a moment's lapse—

it's no wonder the steps appear to lurch up
with no apparent destination.

i peer into the tight frames
of the black and whites wanting to lift out more
than what's customary.

what hurts
is the flat wash of grey licking over the details
as if to make the inadequacies softer, paler than what memory recalls.
even the city seems throttled for silence.
its clever mute presence is wrapped around their shoulders as if to say:

feel me, instead of the ripped silences
taped together at the seams—

23

but the eye travels on through grey
washing over its own greyness
as if searching for the place
where the heart could have entered,
where meaning could still be read.

step by step

Greenwich Village, N.Y., 1994

in the falling evening,
    i hear footsteps
        approaching from behind
and a mixture
    of voices,
        his
overspeaking hers,

        . . . i can take care of myself,
        i ain't *no fuckin' pussy—*

slowing in persistent rain,
i let them pass. her once bolstering voice
falters into silence.
she is careful
to match her strides to his
        brisking
           in and out of light.

reduced
to a fact of disgust and pleasure,

she tilts her head toward the ground.

he is still a man, not yet a cunt,
he assures himself with the brunt of his voice
levied against her.

adroit at denying his epithets, perhaps tonight,
she'll break through to her own sensibility,
to the awareness of his rage and the rage
she has endured
        from the tongues of other men.

gentleman enough, he assures himself
as he carries an umbrella for his *lady,*
whom he can loathe and love
        in the same foul breath.

breach

rifled
by the slow chill of a new york city wind,
i wrap my body tightly in the pale skin
of my down-filled coat and remember
        the narrow passage of childhood:
      its wintered rooms
their dark crust of soot
blotting the walls.

like apparitions,
moving by faint candlelight, we glide
on the almost luminescence that the eye tunnels
toward. drifting from room to room
      on the crackle of linoleum and the hushed *whoosh*
of three-tiered clothing,
hardly a word passes among us.

in clattering cold,
my mother soldiers from work
to home between the two ends of darkness,
and spring will come,
        with its false starts,
before we pass from this season.

      at night,
it is hard to eat
what is already cold and obscured.
               dreamless,
we sleep in our clothes and awaken
in the flat, iced mouth of winter.

meager wishes

i pass the old avenue where
our lives were stitched
        together
as if by the frayed threads of a shoestring,
on its last, for the second time around.

the cobblestones have given way
to time's slow descent and the gravity
of our lives moved forward then back.

at the edge of it all are the simple brick-faced houses, glum,
in their adamantine countenances with their mocking-eye windows
and doorways that take me in like hunger.

on most every street, i can still see *her:*
a thin silhouette shrinking along the walls.
i see *her* in every brown-eyed girl with frizzled hair
and candied gaze. i see *her* in every girlchild who carries
the waddling weight of some other woman's child, mothering,
before she knows the real meaning of this word,
before she knows the meaning of *her* own hard won life.

meager wishes are not enough to make a meal that satisfies,
to make a life that can climb upon itself and rise by its own bright light.

a room full of light

spindles of light
cascade through the bedroom curtains
blue as the iced underbelly of a wintered pond.
        how can you say that—
in the early shadows, the bowl of my breath moves out,
from my sleep-stitched body, a holographic exile from my dreams.
it is more than a wish i have to lift out of this room
where my life hangs like exhaust on the walls.
        there is a part of me that does not want to say this—
every day is a lifetime again it seems: the same room, the same breath,
the same dream that i cannot seem to awaken from.
        . . . and where is this leading—
here in my bowery, i listen to the shades,
the disciples of indigo where i learn to bear the burden
like a condemned man with his blue, blue fingers stuck for ages in his
    blue guitar.
i have no other songs, no notes that lift toward grace or a grander
    scale,
just the thin shale of the black-faced notes that keep playing on in a
    minor key.

if heaven is here . . .

every night,
i turn my face toward the wall and peer out
to where you might be.
i listen
to the call of the river
           churning
      over and over,
            twining,
      as if carrying me along its shoals,
its mossed over rocks   stones on which i would sit
if the tongue of memory would slow a little . . .

     it's the fulsome dark
that tunnels   through grainy images,
steps leading to your door.   i've been here
a hundred nighttimes before   and still, i rush to get in—

sitting on a white stool,
in your white room,
you face me
full on. there is a hole where the television once burned.

    —grandmother,
     what have i come for—
      your own mother paces,
     in silence,
      outside your door.

i can find no meaning to this life
                     after your death.

in this circle of returning,
like salmon pushing up
in a downward stream,
we come again and again,
each time as if unremembered,
like the web of dreams that we thread upon waking,
wanting to know if what's real is real.

how many more currents will we travel before we know . . .

when will this hunger for union cease to swell in my veins,
in the salmonoid recesses of my brain,
bridge to what we were,
to what i am
even in your absence?

      —does the wheel remember its journey
        each time it turns upon itself . . .

it was my silent call that brought you,
lifted you from nothing i know
to my hallowed sphere of dreams.

i recognize your face
as the one you wore
when you believed in your own strength,
when i knew you only as strength:
      name
of what was possible.

going to the well

i dreamed of my father.
he wore his '50s body:
slender, youthful, draped
in silk slacks and a cashmere sweater.
he was all the rage with smooth
finger waves conked over his head
and ray charles–styled shades sitting like blinders
in front of his eyes. i could not read his intent.

when he stood,
he made the shape of cool.

as any child might, i followed him.
he did not see me trailing; he only
saw his own path that led him
from one woman to the next,
and for every one he found, he would fall before her
bearing his face at her feet or knees if she were kneeling.
he would lie there losing himself
to find himself in someone else's need.
it was no wonder that i could recognized this man,
visiting from the realm of the longtime dead,
he who fell into my dream, selfsame
man, who fathered without clear intent.

i had only known him for a day, it seems, before
his earthly stint was up. before i could understand
how it was that i was his child: fruit of his deeds.
it would be many years
of baleful lovers before i could see
my way out of the terrible
pull and drag of losing my own self to them.

in this dream of the lingering adolescence of my father
and his fancy for women, big cars and fine clothes—
his dream of greatness—i could see
how empty he must have felt,
how this vacuousness
must have compelled him to thrust himself
into any woman, willing or not,
without regard for the harvest from his seed.

bastard

every year
at school, the white index cards came
asking for name,
address and names of parents.

i had no father—

. . . didn't know what name to put for his.
my mother always told me to write
deceased, and every year, i'd have to remember
my deceased father whom i'd never known.

by the sixth grade, i could manage *deceased*
myself. by the tenth, a simple line
drawn through would suffice, even though, i knew
by then, my father was not dead.

> *o mary, mother of jesus, what is the burden of a holy ghost—*

my mother mirrored our stream of love and hate
with sideways glances assailing his image
flounced on the couch in my wrinkled dress,
the eddying indifference, the burden of her maternity,
the unmention of his name. we waded through bearing
the yoke of our blood. and the father—

what of his blood—was he a dark jehovah
whose name i could not call—was i
the seed despised, the child
thrown away, as atonement for his sins—

> *o father . . . why hast thou forsaken me—*

my father, like a spirit unseen,
does not come when called.

birthmark

my mother pulled me from the fire raging between her legs.
by the top hairs, she hauled my freshly minted body onto hers.

i was not the would-be boy-child of her dreams,
but the sad mirror in whose eyes she saw
the road along which she had already traveled.

the female road comes without promise of fair weather,
without promise of a face welcomed at the breakfast table
unless she, even if only through some sleight of hand,
brings along a male child   to mask
                              her own worthiness.

my brother passed through gates whose fires i had already eaten;
they lay hidden in my belly smoldering,
        waiting for that least bit of kindling
     that might ignite the belief
                              in   my own heart.

apple picking

looking back over the years, mother,
i see the tips of our lives
bend toward each other.
each tipped bough flickers
like light
        refracted.

through the palimpsest of my life
                    superimposed
over the laminated face
of my school desk,

i sit solitary
in a row
of seats
under the blank eye of the window.

as if by stealth,
the crumpled folds
of crayoned images
emerge from between my textbook pages.

it's a simple sketch
in purples, blues and greens.
a buoyant yellow is lacking.
here and there, red bleeds through.

in the center,
the fructifying flesh
of an adam and eve
finds the firm, round fruit of their sex.

i have fruit
without knowing the tree

from which it fell. with a vagabond
hunger, i am eaten to the core.

my mother eats.

her room fills with apple cores. her life
recedes like a promise of paradise.

. . . he is not the first man
to burnish the apple,

you are not the first woman
to reach for the tender core . . .

i am the child
turned away at the gate—

i wanted to pry your arms
from around the lusty heart
                        of adam,

but
with each caught breath,
you opened yourself, even more,
for that one cataclysmic jolt
that would suspend
the nightmare of our lives,
momentarily, above your head
while eternity poured through you
              like light through a veil.

sunstroke

summer's alabaster sun
blanches the house
and swells the air.

the sidewalk undulates.

on the second floor, the newly wed,
high-yellow, flat-chested woman
halts the iron mid-wrinkle, props
it near the pop-bottle sprinkler.

creped in her nylon slip,
she walks toward the window;
each rounded buttock shifts
of its own accord.

she pulls the dangle of hair
back from her face. the smell
of purple sweat and red clay
rises from her arm pits.
   she remembers
                  his sex
              forced
between her legs,
the fire of her womb.
she bends and leans out
on her bright palms.

into the thick heat
she yells. her shrill voice
parts the stagnant air
and lifts the red clay child
like summer lightning
                to her feet.

she runs in a half start
                toward home.

the light arrives at an oblique angle

the light fuses through slight ice crystals
stuck like postage stamps to the glass.
my breath, heavy from stitching
the darkened lining of my dreams,
folds in on itself in the chilled hours of the morning air.
although i am bundled for the outdoors
and sandwiched between layers of blankets,
my thin nine-year-old body shudders,
unable to call forth its own warmth. all is silent
except for the fallen torsos of my mother
and brother, layered in their coats and jackets, exiled in sleep.
the day begins like a steep ledge. it will be a long while
before we can climb over, before spring-light will wash
down the sooted walls, and show us our faces.

necessary kindling

it is said that we are souls
who return to life as if upon a wheel. . . .

this morning, under the spell
of a second sleep,
i saw my brother
wearing his ten-year-old body.
he seemed quite innocent,
unable to distinguish himself
from the things belonging to the world.

how are we to be in the world without being of it—

even in that light sleep,
i wanted to touch him,
to extend my adult ephemeral dream-hand
toward that child who was my brother,
who was still eating everything
as if it meant his life.

waking, i remembered how our lives
seemed hinged once,
how at ten,
he was beginning to act out an unspeakable rage
that would seal his fate for years.

i can't imagine this life
beginning again
or regaining what has been lost.
i have tried more than once
to reawaken an innocence
that some say lies sleeping in our hearts.

i have grown impatient,
unwilling to wade through
another bevy of tomorrows
before finding the necessary kindling
that will light our way home.

stasis

in the year of my 15th summer,
when my body
was not of much use to boys,
i lay on my bed
listening to the radio
while the sky
ticked toward autumn.

lulled
by the monotony
of the d.j. and the endless trail of song,
i drifted to the memory
of the visiting peeks boy.

in his secret trips to my room,
he forced his blunt sex between my legs.

i listened to the hollow
echo of my unsounded body

and gagged on the sour smell
of unripened sex.

in the summer heat, i imagine
the cool body of a pool, surrounded
by chain link and barbed wire;
ron peeks climbs up and over.

i see him break the black body
of the pool.   his arms flail.
he churns its blackness
into froth and foam.
this time,
    it
        swallows him.

under dark clouds
and feeble sky, i release my grip
on the fence, drop my hands

to my sides as i listen to the slow
easy lap of the water
nipping inside my head.

papa's maybe

my mother telephones at an early hour.
her solicitous voice belies
a present danger.

already, my stomach, my feeling brain
has begun to draw into a gastric knot—

she's received a call from my daughter's
boyfriend, the father of my soon-to-be grandchild.
. . . seems he's carrying doubt about the paternity
of *her* child. he wants to back out
'cause his friend
done told him *it can't be his;* done told him
how *them bitches will lie on a man.*
just cause he put his dick in her,
she wanna lay that on him.

never mind that she has made several trips
back to see him, has abstained from dating
other boys, has written enough
letters to start a paper mill. all the while, i listen
to his words sniggering through my mind
as he joins the long list of men
who want to cast doubt on their paternity,
on her fidelity,
                    while he absconds
with his makeshift integrity intact.

my own mother had to take my father to court,
had to stand before the judge and spill her guts.
with only her word as shield, she had to prove
she was not a slut in order to be heard,
to be granted two cents in his name.

let it be told: it's still the woman's blame
for bringing a child into the world.

thirty-five and a half weeks

at thirty-five and a half weeks,
my daughter's womb,
a half-somersaulted pear,
caught with the bulb of its butt
upended, rests in the cradle of her hips,
the weft of its ligaments
                    coming undone.

on this, the start of her weekly visits,
the doctor reports
the baby's head is decidedly down;
it has begun to assume the position
for making its descent.

i wonder what it could know or smell
that sends it down into the bowels
of its mother's body seeking that harrowing passage
where it once entered, as a half-being,
at the end of consensual pleasure.

does part of its catacombed brain
bear a map of an intricate pathway
to the world once experienced
as part of some others' bodies—

who among us can imagine this—

not i, who seem of the not born;
not my daughter, who seems parasited
by her child's desire to enter life
from the mouth
that lies between the portals of piss and shit;
not the child, whose fetal memory is flooded
at birth by the fiery burn of air into its lungs
as it cries out in its first chorus
of the humans' song: suffering to be born.

the whipping

for Robert Hayden

under the scintillating heat of a sepia sun,
the grandmother, her mahogany skin shimmering
when she walks, fills the shirtwaist seams of her dress,
the lower half a sashayed mass of turbulent floral patterns,
tossed as if in a storm, moves through the shotgun
arrangement of rooms to the edge of the porch,
                              to the lean-to sapling
    wavering its thin tentacled branches
beneath her urgent and fleshed palms.

she snaps off a switch and deflowers its sprigs.
carefully, she peels back the green husk
down to the stark wet white and begins
to move, rapid fire, back through the house.
she seizes the small boy waiting in knee socks,
sunday shorts and dark bow tie
by the shank of his arm.

already, a profuse sweat has begun to gleam on her skin.
half mumbling, she sermonizes about what she'd told him
to do: to stay put, to stay clean and quiet.

like a frenzied musician, she flails on his bright flesh
already red and blistering. she holds him
where he cannot squirm,
cannot get loose from her grip
'til her arms, spent wands,
                              hang limply at her sides.

son

at the blood gate,
at the howling birth mouth,
   i listened for you
day and night—

before i could name you,
before you could bear the lips
of your father whispering his hushed prayers
into your ears, i knew you were not the one
i had hoped for, the clever child
of my dreams, the firstborn boy who would carry a name
and defend sisters with clenched fists.

in the harrowing moments,
you could not see
how you looked in that unerring light burning
above our heads or how i tried to be proud,
brave in the dizzying aftermath
as your cheese-covered body was lifted
from mine prematurely, blue startled lungs
on helpless fire.
you were too weak to be held
or put to breast   so cold and contorted
on the metal scales.

over the days, i listen
for your small hungry voice:
an echo from the nursery.
i recognize all voices
                as not yours.

with little regard for the dead umbilicus,
you sleep through all hours
as if you have no desire for food,
as if my blood will still keep you alive.

in my useless hours,
milk is a chore.
my engorged breasts become burdens.

i stroke their veined surfaces, and pump
the brown snouts of the raw aureoles. i pour out
this thin food.

in the incubator, dressed in goggles
and a white cap, the glaze of the bilirubin light
vacuums the excess white cells . . .
                    you lie: a motorcycle rider
spilled from his bike. the nurses
tend you like a lab specimen,
                              a cultured life.

i want to hold you in my arms.

i want your tiny pale lips at my
swelled breasts, to feel you draw this agony
away, to bear your routing mouth, the bald
ridges of your gums, to become more
than what can be evidenced by the turning of a phrase,

but sleep is the only hunger you know,
the only mother you squint your eyes toward
even when i pinch your bruised heel, and lift
your tired mouth again to my breasts.

making the grade

ragweed, dandelion spikes and spent leaves
tumble absentmindedly in grass
already wagging its tongue toward autumn.
what can i say now,
          sunday is sure to come—

trash cans, with their broken shoulders,
lean onto themselves at every corner.
at every corner, i want to throw away these dingy
strips of second-grade paper streaked with blue lines,
thin as a coward's veins, with letters that turn their backs
on grammar rules, forming words their own way,
the way they might be spelled on mars or a furthest planet.

thinking on the hard-knuckled, table-rappin' work
of my mama as she drilled those letters across my tongue
like urgent soldiers, i know i can't go home,
can't take my poor man's list of misspelled words home.

i study the mouths of the cans,
their apparent hunger for my strips,
          each kissed with a flag of red;
i regard their need and consider my own:
                    no more whippin's from mama.

sunday

raising the borrowed ladder, my son
and i clip the upturned lip of the gutters
stuffed like gluttons with pine straw
and the dried remnants of leaves.

being the elder,
i press the splintered wood
between my fingers as if to guide
the ascending rungs into the grey mouth
                                        of the sky.

in this moth-eaten air,
the yellow leaves
scatter among the blades
of grass like willing bones.
our jackets lift
like an anxious bird's tail.

                        i cannot fly.
i am anchored to the earth's
brown moss, but he ascends
the paint-stained rungs
        in his lithe body
                        like one
born again.

as tentative wings,
his feet light
against that uneven ground.

like a proud roof ornament
seeking the proper direction,
he struts the full measure
of the gables,
                end to end,
turning, barely kneeling
to counter the slant edge.

i marvel at his ascension,

the nimble way he hangs
between heaven and earth

as though he belonged
                    to neither.

atonement

son gone,
glad for him to go.
day done, shed no tears.
night begins at father's door.

uneven tide

i can't get to sleep
thinking son
the whole night.
he says he's *lost,*
so i imagine him churning in some sea.

long before the rounded edge has found him,
he sinks and spins crossing the invisible,
zone after zone. he has no time on his hands.

my mind goes numb; i've hit the glass wall.
he is on the other side bobbing, gulping.
i go slack before the break.

the shards are hot;
the light bleeds—

the three-pronged edge of my anger
fails to lift him.

his sea is thick tonight.
the current carries me
to where we were once connected.

                              i am afraid—

my womb remembers
his zygote bobbing,
fishtail climbing,
and the twisted cables of blood
flowing near without ever touching,

nor can i touch him now.
he's mired off the coast
like a derelict hull,
blue and turning bluer.

on the hill
stands his father.

what little blood he has
drains through his feet.

instead of saving
a son, i must carry
the burial song,
humming it in place of his name.

on the fire trail

for S.H.A.

i have traveled
cross-country
on greyhound
while dreaming,
in the bordering states, son,
of a reunion
with you.

      after 7 years
      of separation,
      we walk
      the fire trail
      spiraling through
      thorned
      thicket
      and summer heat
      lifting
      slowly
      through
      the
      berkeley
      foothills.

today
we have set aside
for berry picking.

      under a
      weightless
      sky,
      we drift
      along the ridge
      like the warmed
      vapors rising
      along
      the slopes.

watching
for poison
oak,
you tilt
your man–sized
body
to the brush,
straining your arms
out into the dense tangle
of branches,
some twisted,
some dangled
as if by thread
& pick the best
of what was hidden
from view.

everyone
who passes
devours fruit
whose own thorns
cannot protect it.
on this day
set aside for berry picking,
i can hardly
believe
i now must stand behind
and watch, as you
take your turn
at using great care,
not wanting
to destroy
that which gives
of itself
to you.